In That Day

In That Day

Poems by
May Williams Ward

Illustrated with her block prints

With a Foreword by Bruce Cutler

THE UNIVERSITY PRESS OF KANSAS
Lawrence, Manhattan, Wichita, London

For my husband,
Merle C. Ward

Acknowledgments

Since the poems in *In That Day* were chosen from very early as well as later years, some of the periodicals and anthologies listed have changed hands or are out of print. I have forgotten some, for my scrapbooks are not complete. But I do thank and do hope others may recall the quick and the dead, listed below.

Thanks to the special poetry magazines: *The Harp, Poetry, Kansas Magazine, Kansas Quarterly, The Georgia Review, Prairie Schooner, Kaleidograph, University of Missouri at Kansas City Review, The Lyric, The Lyric West, Voices, Seesaw, Contemporary Verse, Bozart, Musical Leader.*

Also, thanks to *Commonweal, Nation, Life, Household, Good Housekeeping, Ladies' Home Journal, Saturday Evening Post, Child Life, Christian Science Monitor,* Kansas City *Star,* New York *Times,* New York *Herald Tribune,* Washington *Star,* Denver *Post, The Christian.*

Some of these poems have been reprinted in anthologies and textbooks. All are used here with permission of the copyright owners.

I am especially grateful to Bruce Cutler for his counsel in selecting and arranging the poems in this book.

M.W.W.

Foreword

This book by May Williams Ward is the first collection of poems to be published by the University Press of Kansas. Two of the goals of the Press since its inception have been to publish works of scholarly or artistic importance, and to publish works which meaningfully interpret life in Kansas and mid-America. It is particularly pleasant to see both goals achieved in the publication of this volume of Mrs. Ward's poetry.

My first meeting with May Ward came in the editorial offices of the *Kansas Magazine* on a stormy February afternoon in 1956. May was then serving as a consulting editor of the magazine, and we began to talk about poetry as though it were the most natural thing to do on a snowy February afternoon in Kansas. As we talked, I soon realized that people and poets who were mostly names to me were both names and personalities to her. Over the years she had formed acquaintanceships with a large number of writers, including Harriet Monroe, Harold Vinal, Robert Hillyer, Sara Teasdale, Edward Arlington Robinson, Stephen Vincent Benét, and Edwin Markham, as well as with editors William Allen White, Roy Roberts, and the indefatigable Haldeman-Julius. In a magazine which she edited during the twenties, *The Harp*, she had published work by Amy Lowell, John Farrar, Louise Bogan, as well as by Robinson, Hillyer, and many others.

May has lately been "grounded" (as she says) with her husband in their home in Wellington, Kansas. But her conversations have continued as buoyant as ever. She has continued to write and publish, to give lecture recitals and conduct workshops, even though her trips to editorial meetings have had to be curtailed. Wellington is still enlivened by her regular book reviews in the *Daily News*, and the newspaper has done as much to inform its readers about contemporary writing as any other newspaper in the United States.

May Williams was born in 1882 in Holden, Missouri. Her mother, Sarah Smith Williams, was the daughter of Captain Reuben Smith, a naturalized British citizen who had come to the Kansas Territory in 1857 to help the abolitionist cause during the era of Border Warfare. Her father, George Williams, soon moved his family from Missouri to Osawatomie, Kansas. In spirit, Osawatomie was still very much John Brown's community, and freed slaves worked farms there. May graduated first in her class in high school; and in 1905 she graduated with a major in mathematics from the University of Kansas, where she had been elected to Phi Beta Kappa. She married Merle Ward, who had been born in his grandfather's log cabin in Geuda Springs, Kansas, the son of a former Star Route Pony Express rider, and whom she had met while both were students in Lawrence. The marriage took place in Osawatomie in 1908 in the Congregational Church built by John Brown and his brother-in-law, S. L. Adair, and John Brown's grandniece was the organist. Years later, when the stone pergola was built over the John Brown cabin in Osawatomie, one of May's poems was sealed in the cornerstone. Considering these beginnings, the changes in American life and literature which were to occur during the lives of these two people were enormous. The Wards proved equal to all of them.

While May wrote from her early years, her career as a serious writer may be said to have begun in 1925. In that year Mrs. Edward McDowell, the composer's widow, invited May to join the colony of writers and artists over which she presided. William Allen White, one of May's sponsors, continued to encourage her. She became editor for six years of *The Harp,* already referred to, and a group of seven of her poems was published in *Poetry* in 1927. Edwin Markham nominated her for membership in the Poetry Society of America. She wrote and published thousands of poems, book reviews, and articles in subsequent years, and in 1937 she won the Poetry Society of America Award for "Dust Bowl," a group of poems which later were published in the New York *Times.* Some collections of her poetry appeared, also. In 1929 *Seesaw* was published by the Bozart Press and was exhibited at the Century of Progress in Chicago in 1933. In the same year May hand-printed an elegant edition of *In Double Rhythm,* a collection of poems and original block prints which was widely sought by libraries. A book of collected poems entitled *From Christmastime to April,* winner of the *Kaleidograph* book publication contest, appeared in 1938. *Choral Speech* appeared in 1945, and *Wheatlands* in 1954. She privately printed her autobiography, *No Two Years Alike,* in 1960. And during the thirty-six years of its existence, the *Kansas Magazine* (now the *Kansas Quarterly*) received her assistance as contributor, poetry editor, and consulting editor.

In her adult life in Kansas, May has seen the coming and going of such poetic movements as imagism, surrealism, formalism, and concretism, to name a few. Her poetry has steered its own steady course. In any collection of poems published over a period of some fifty years, there are bound to be changes and developments. But May's outstanding feeling for language, her deft use of metaphor and imagery, and her intuitive grasp of the relationships between word, sound, and line have always remained constant. Anyone confronted with the task of assembling and editing a selection of her poems would find it difficult to arrive at a final set of choices. For me, it would have been impossible without the kind assistance of a number of people, including Dorothy Diacon, Jo Hoglan, Peggy Greene, Virginia Scott Miner, and Will Moses, to all of whom I am much indebted for help.

As these poems make clear, what we truly know is what, near the end of a long and fruitful life, we can leave for others to share with us. What I most value in May Ward's poetry is a way of seeing that reveals in the apparently uncompromising contours of our life the forms of the unexpected, the outlines of a reality which only the living tissue of the poet's words can manifest. It is a pleasure to share in that reality.

Bruce Cutler

Contents

III

I

In That Day

And every island fled away
and the mountains were not found
nor were the rivers found;

the cities and the wheat-white plains
were swallowed underground
and the void sucked in the ground;

the oceans turned to flying mist
and vanished without sound
after that first great sound

and the race of men went with the rest
as Jahweh willed it should.
It was fitting that it should.

There was a nothingness of dark
where once the planets stood,
where once they sloped and stood,

and God looked on His handiwork
and saw that it was good—
the clean clear space was good.

Last Man, Last Bird

The rain begins. The sea begins
To flatten under flattening sky.
A gull goes by.
He cuts a scalloping of curves
Above defeated waves
Flat since the rain began.

But the gull flies on.

A man lies on
The beach, awaiting a signal. He,
Bored with the flat monotony,
Suddenly feels unable to bear
The void left there
Of grace or motion in sky or sea
Since the gull is gone.
So he hoops his arms in a dive, for one
Short interval to see curves again.

But the ripples he makes are dying down.

The shore regained, he lies down again,
Another flatness under the rain
Like sea and sky since the rain began.

The catastrophic rain goes on
Till every curve is forever gone.

Psalm of Fear

How can a woman keep her son
That he shall not die?
Even when hid beneath her heart
There were foes to fight
And at birth precarious gates to pass.
Since then
She has snatched him from death in multiple guises.
Death wheeled,
Knife-edged,
Green-poisonous,
Hot;
From death cliff-tall,
Sea-deep.
And now he has entered the world of men.
Great winged death he cozens now
And flirts with war.
How can a woman keep her son
That he shall not die?

Partly a Sadness

Now when the snow slips over the hill,
Now when the dark comes while it is day,
There is a strangeness when all grows still,
Partly a sadness, partly a thrill,
    Someway.

It is then we remember the wrong we do,
It is then we wonder what makes a cloud,
And where children have gone whom we used to know,
Lost from us now in some far-off crowd.

It is partly a sadness, partly a thrill,
When the great white snow comes over the hill,
And we think our thoughts in the dark and the chill,
It is partly a sadness, partly a thrill,
    Someway . . .

The Tree and I

Over the tree the breeze blew.
Leaves moved gently, the birds knew
Now was the time for sweetest song;
They piped and caroled the day long.
    (I was a girl.)
The breeze blew.

Into the tree the rain fell.
Buds of fruit began to swell;
Birds peeped bright-eyed out of the nest,
Leaves hung glossy and calm, at rest.
    (I was a woman.)
The rain fell.

Athwart the tree the lightning flashed
Branches and nests of the great crown crashed.
From the broken trunk leaves sprang anew,
But a long time after, and few, how few . . .
    (I was a widow.)
The lightning flashed.

Jets Over the Wheatlands

A people of our wheat's color
Or no-color, wholesome, good
As bread-flour fresh from the local miller,
Our lives used to be broad
Peaceful and smooth as the plain. But not any longer.
Jet-planes zoom nearby
Pushed on their sudden flight by fiery fingers
And all our sons fly.
They fly the world. Our thoughts go speeding
    with them
Through dawns, through stormy black,
Through rainbows, and over painted seas and cities—
Speeding and circling back.
Not again will we have wheat-colored days and quiet.
Thunderclaps have called
Our sons and us to be part of
    the broken prismatic riot
Of the colorful,
Pitiful, wonderful world.

Illusion of a Gift Conferred

Something signals: Watch for more.
Someone vague seems to run before
to dive in waters fructified
by elementals in the pied
murk and light.

Then a small treasure streaked with bright
may be brought up to the surface world.
A poem, curiously whorled.

The seeming others can only be
myself diving down in dark of me,
yet when the poem comes
is it truly all mine? It feels to be
more—
as if a sea in primal tidal power
conferred a shell on a sterile sandy shore.

Indian Summer

There is an instant of rest for the heavy-driving heart
between the thrust and clutch of one beat's ending
and another's start.
If we listen, there is a click of silence
between the tick and tock of the clock.

Even so in poised breath-holding Indian summer
time flutters free
for a season's moment, from weight of what is finished,
what must be.

Decrescendo

The arc of the moon in waning
Is smooth as her upward swing.
Autumn and quiet winter
Flow gently down from spring.
Roses are calm through cycles
Of petal and petal dust
But men grow old resentfully
And only because they must.

Reluctant Return

The town flows down the foothill flank like water.
Roofs seem rocks firm in the wavering slant.
Riffles of shadow in between look haunted
to eyes of the man starting the long descent
into his past, into the unremembered
and the too well remembered. Halfway down
he stumbles into her courtyard as into a whirlpool
to drown.

Ancient Enemy

This man in winter sweats a dream of hell
and it is Dante's fearful hell of ice.
His family is cursed. Ten storms compelled
his great-grandfather's pain and sacrifice
at Valley Forge. The Civil War stockades,
a sleety trench in France, an Arctic dune
and wild Korea, all were ambuscades
where cold could hide to strike his kinfolk down.
With horror now he reads of buses stalled
and hunters lost in winter, even today.
He dreams recurrently of being called
by the ancient enemy in a foreknown way—
> To pierce through ice where the cliff of hell begins,
> Cling there and freeze forever for his sins.

They Talk of Time

Rose mentions roses and today, ephemeral;
Fossil shell
Speaks thousand years and thousand years since glacier-fall;

And sky proclaims the eon-marks on every star
Where wild force tore
And still is tearing life to death, near to far.

Two Old Women

Old Woman on a Fine Day

Scatter back, skim forth,
Skitter through the blue,
Don't blame you, birds, this fine day!
Guess I'll zig a few
Zags with you along the breeze
Not going anywhere;
Then float down to rest again
In my wheelchair.

Old Woman on a Snowy Day

I am as snow,
Sometimes cruel, blizzard-cold, nagging,
Oftener I go touching in my thought
Cheeks of children, strangers, lovers,
Lightly as snowflakes flying low.

Writer

While bitter seeds scatter from the ruptured pod Earth
As wind words are a-mutter: *death and death and death*

While other too-ripe planets fall apart in rot
And spilled juice of comets spurts out hot

When lightnings roll tide-like west to east and back
And time's wheel slipping sidewise jars the cosmic clock—

Someone will cling with one hand to a fragment bound for hell
While the other hand scrawls shorthand, reporting on it all.

A writer in his element, this "beat" his final glory:
His the one first-hand account of the great, the ultimate story.

The Leaves

In tigerhide, in appleskin,
or in flamingo breast
autumn leaves are dressed.

As sawtooth shell, as long lance,
as trefoil, as grape,
autumn leaves are shaped.

Sticky, smooth, sensuous,
or thorned as with sharpened steel
are autumn leaves to feel.

And they must fall. They must fall
but not before glory:
their story, man's story.

A woman walked over her threshold
to see the leaves and the grass
and time going by.

II

Spring Day in Kansas

This is a day like days in a storybook,
With glitter in the air that glorifies
The edge and tip of every leaf, and lies
In pools of mirror strangeness on the brook.
Pale trees are deeply shadowed with the look
Of rendezvous, and clouds like turrets rise.
This is a day for knights and their emprise.
Treasure seems probable in any nook.

And I am not a changeling in the tale.
My ears feel pointed. I can talk in rhyme
Today, and know what birds say in their song.
I'll find a nest, I know, here in the swale,
And over this next hill that I shall climb,
The lover I have waited for so long.

Wet Summer

The hollyhocks are ten feet tall,
The larkspur deeply colored;
Once dried-up lakes are nearly full
And shelter half-grown mallard.

The ivy overflows its urn.
The elm which long drouth withered
Revives, and on each branch-tip burn
Bright leaflets, newly feathered.

The crows have grown not quite so rude,
The robins, fat as butter.
They chant a new Beatitude:
    Blessed be water!

Tornado Over Kansas

Tin-toned bells clappered,
Sirens spiraled shrieks.
Storm vultures sharpened beaks
While men ran and scattered
Into cellars, into ditches.
The great storm split boles,
Sucked up roofs, blasted holes,
And stripped the wheat to rags from riches.

Sleet Storm

In darkness, in riot of darkness
Moisture of sky started
To freeze into cloud-wide slush
But the wind whiplashed
What might have been drops into shards
Chunks, lumps and barbed-wire shreds.

In darkness, in riot of darkness
Was contained then, riot of whiteness.
The ice-stones battered each other
And roofs and earth in a smother
Of shriek-thick black, of white-whirl stress
In darkness, in riot of darkness.

Then all at once it was over;
Nothing left but a cover
Of innocent-looking glassy beads
Over the morning-sunny streets
And half unbelievable memories
Of riots of whiteness in darkness.

Lakescape: Theme with Variations

Butterflies
flitter
and flutter
at the lakeside
in desultory enterprise.

To flatter
even the young and fair,
the lake mirrors
in shimmers
faces leaning there
until ripples begin to run.
Fleeter than whispers they slide,
pewter in shadow,
copper in sun.

And oh hear the blackbird,
fluter
of ecstasy in his song;
and there the lake's lovely
floater,
the swan.

Even in Worlds Like Ours

If quietly the lavender
Or if the orchid-blue
Of lilacs makes a subtle stir
Of scent, there lifts a slow
Awareness to delight and then
Perception once again
That emotion need not fly
Jet-powered, nor be neon-flamed.
Even in worlds like ours
It may rise slowly, like perfume
From small and simple flowers.

Autumn Leaves Are Not As Birds

In bronze-brown tones
of a rooster's tail
or in red of his crest
leaves may be dressed.

Closely crowding
upon tree roosts
tiered in rings
leaves may cling—

But they cannot stay.
Fowl fly down
and back next day.

Leaves fly one way.

Daylight Moon

The sun keeps making a clamor and confusion
of going down. Volcano red
erupts across the blue and mauve collision
of cloudbanks spread
overhead.

But far withdrawn in another part of the heavens
a pure and perfect curve is dimly seen.
Within a float of indistinct translucence
the moon, faint green,
swims serene.

Three Views of Time From a Garden

Time flutters prettily close at hand,
ephemeral over ephemeral rose,
and inconsequentially toys
with breeze in trees.
It moves irregularly
along with the nows of bloom and not-bloom
hastened or held back by weathers.

Beyond flower beds is a wall
of pitted boulders.
Time has lumbered elephantishly backward
here, to the glacial age.
Once-upon-a-time-long-ago
is visible, tangible here,
static, arrested.

And future time?
In the sky this sunset, portents.
Wild color slashes there
and thunder-violence threatens.

Slow Rain

A slow rain slides murmurously
down the slope of the shingles
humping a little over the edge of the eaves
the way a brook humps over its stones.
There are only muted jingles
when it falls to the pebbly trough scoured clear of leaves.

This night persuades to quiet sleep
even the heaviest-hearted
with intermittent music and soundless swell
of coolness. Then lying dreams come on
pretending that never have parted
lover and lover. Pretending that all is well.

Lightning

Lightning is a crazy tree,
a tree uprooted, inverted.
Branches flare from its trunk in a wink
and twigs explode from the branches.
Even the maddest for speed in a speed-mad world
know this tree grows too fast,
and that its fruit is fear.

Garden Wedding

Lilies float their fragrance over the arbor.
From the wineglass elm is poured a wavering, wide
Pool of shadow. Lilacs jewel the border
With silver hearts for leaves on the moonward side.
Violins from the brookside terrace are sending
Quivering notes over quivering water flowing,
Scarcely breaking the stillness. But there is thunder
Rolling in hearts of the parents, thunder of knowing
That the child of this home this garden this love
    this pride
Is child no more. They are coming, bridegroom
    and bride.

Three Poems

The Neglected

Rich sky harvest lies uncut
by the withdrawn sickle moon.
Bodies too are curved but what
of that if there be none
to use them? There is need of one
to sharpen sickles (with what whetstone?)
to appraise the yields in fields forgot
and to bring the good wheat home.

So Long Incomplete

Mortise and tenon
Slippered foot
Arrow in quiver
Buried root
Arch with keystone
Seeded ground
Spire in vast void—
There is found
Nothing single.
Each is key
In, of, another—
Except me.

Unsent Letter to a Son About to Marry

Oh how subtle, oh how good
not to urge against her wooden
taut reluctance to be loved.
Woo her partly, gently. Leave
violence until her own
ripens full, demanding pain.

Sharing then true marriagehood
oh how subtle, oh how good
her warmth of blessing you for this
giving, taking, pain turned bliss.

III

"MY·LITTLE·SISTER"
·HAD·HAP-
PINESS,SYMBOLIZED
BY·A·WREATH···THE
SNAKE·PORTRAYS·THE
OTHER·SISTER'S·ENVY.
MAY·WREATHS
BE·YOURS

My Little Sister

My little sister had everything.
　　Everything in the world—
Blue eyes, dimples, pink cheeks,
　　And her hair curled.

She played forward at basketball
　　And shot ducks from cover.
She had a sweet rose-colored hat
　　And a tall lover.

All her life she had everything;
　　Plenty and more than plenty.
She did not need a perfect death—
　　Death at twenty.

In the Grain

Your words move upon silence
as a boat made of salt-soaked planks
moves upon the sea,
like something under which for long
its elements had lain.

Your words move upon silence,
as if soaked with silence,
the best of them impregnated
with silence in the grain.

The Garrulous One

We were seatmates but scarely speechmates during the flight
after steep rise from earth-green into cloud-white.
He was boringly garrulous. I kept snobbishly still.
Mea culpa.

He saw through me, yet thanked me with good will:
You were kind to let me run on about nothing, weather and such.
Where I came from talking is rationed, and often means too much,
he said.

And I remembered then a tenseness over the town
where he embarked. Above it, prison walls looked down.

Two Questions

Can This Be Our Dan?

When this Marine came back from Vietnam
His dog friend's patient wondering was ended
But his barks and leapings up at Daniel's knees
Grew tiresome, so Dan kicked him, not offended
But casually and callously; and then
When Spot came crawling back, kicked him again.

What For?

Today my best beloved went to war.
I bought a new red hat. What for?

I Prayed a Miracle Down

I prayed a miracle down.
When one late perfect rose
Opened long after time
In my garden close,
I prayed: Let winds be stopped
By my latticed gate;
Let frost find the wall too high;
Let Autumn wait.

And they crouched like beasts barred out
For a week and a week and a day
For the lifetime of the rose.

I forgot to pray
That the flower might never fade.

Counting Sheep

Slowly, gently, the drowsy sheep
Gather their hooves and softly leap
Over the low and mossy wall.
None of them stumble, none of them fall.
One, two, three, four . . .
More and more, more and more,
Coming down to the easy turn
Cool with shadow and sweet with fern,
Dim as shadows themselves, they go
Over the wall, slow, slow . . .
Seven, eight, nine, ten . . .
Twelve, twenty . . . Begin again,
Though nobody knows and nobody cares
How the tally of counting fares.
But no one can keep from counting on—
Another lamb coming, another gone,
Twenty, thirty, forty-nine . . .
Over the wall, a rhythmic line
Curved as a wave or a bending tree.
Over the wall the fold must be.
I am a shadow with shadowy sheep.
Rocking over a wall, to sleep.

After Rock and Danger

I live on a plain so I had to climb a mountain
To see just what was there.
I edged past a waterfall and a crag, uncertain
If there were an inch to spare,
And sat on a ledge half hid by a foggy curtain.
My seat had a backrest of air.

I found it good, this knowing of rock and danger
After the placid ring
Of prairie horizons. Water the daring plunger
And water calm in a spring
Are kin to me, both. And suddenly out of my wonder,
Out of my joy, apprehending both over and under,
I began to sing!

We Read John Donne Together

Now I am gone (but never wholly gone)
may you sleep breathing gently, not in tears.
Be comforted to know that we still are one,
could it be otherwise after all these years?

Now I am gone, sleep richly. I will bless
you now as then for your giving heart. And when
you dream, "dream me some happiness"—
somehow I will dream it to you again.
I will, I will, dream it to you again.

In Church

From an oblique angle
a certain elder's profile
looks like a satyr's.
Straight ahead in the choir
a woman's face embodies peace.

Girls Dancing Together, 1914

My roommate dances like flame in the wind;
I, more like stiff wires bending.
We sway together with arms entwined,
both of us pretending.

Far away is her misty glance.
She dreams of her soldier lad,
and I pretend I am clasped as we dance
by the lover I never have had.

Sometimes

The red rose tree must stay put,
anchored by its roots
but its yesterday-petals seek to fly;
they flutter wing-like
and sometimes a breeze
lifts them upward instead of down.
They momentarily move
in a long curve.
    Redbirds in flight.
And sometimes redbirds in flight
are roses with wings.

Threefold

In the day, in the twilight, at night
I remember, remember, remember.
In the day, for its glory is light,
Your radiant zest I remember.
When twilight comes down, gray-feathered dove,
Your intimate, quiet moods haunt me.
And love,
In the night made for love, I remember.
Remember, remember, remember.

Love Me, But Not Too Much

Love me a little, not too much
For much-loved ones must lose
Their molten dangerous selves in such
Fixed molds as their lovers choose.

I must spill over like white-hot steel
Sometimes, which none dare touch;
I cool, to melt again . . . You will
Love me? But not too much?

To One Gone

I thought I should not be happy again but I'm nearly happy
here underneath our wineglass elm which is never so heavily leaved
but that pieces of sky show here and there in scalloped patches.
I am almost happy, holding at last this book by you, beloved.

My elbows lean on this table you made for me with only a hand ax;
it teeters a little on yellowish stones we carted up from the brook
to pave as with gold uneven blocks this our private heaven,
a place of such joy that some remains soaked into me and the book.

Young Soldier and His Enemy

We were taught in training camp
To stab stiff straw-stuffed manikins
With fierce cries. A mood of hate
For the enemy was urgently
Demanded.
We pretended.
But at the front the enemy
At first was only a dim streak
Near the horizon, negligible.
When we saw a few strangers later, on small forays
They looked like boys.
Like boys too we threatened each other
And backed away.

I wonder, for I keep dreaming
The same dream at the beginning
Each time, but enlarging, changing.

In the dream it is moontime sometimes,
More times dark. I climb down a ladder

In an ancient well, at first fearfully.
My enemy close behind me and above me
Steps on my fingers.

Then in later dreams we stopped
Crowding each other and went on down
Through iron-red and ocherous clays
Through limestones and mica-bright strata
And shell-strewn rocky remnants
Of what long-vanished seas
And animosities?

And oh last night in the dream we went very deep
Descending far and late
Past granites and lavas and fossil-beds.
We went side by side on the ladder then.
Did we ever feel hate?
We went as children, almost as twins.
And in the clear water at bottom of the well
Saw two faces reflected.
Which was my face,
Which was his?

Marine's Wife

No more reason to lie awake tonight
than other nights, I tell myself, but know
it is not so.

It was midnight here three hours ago.
What hours of struggle there?
How do you fare?

At last you answer, in or over air;
at last diminished urgency
lets you through to me,

your message wordless, strong. It feels to be
that danger passes, tension is less tight.
It is almost over now. Not quite.
I shall sleep, later tonight.

Song for Midnight Vigils

Now let your restlessness smooth to rest
    Go to sleep—
Let rise and fall of your gentled breast
    In sleep
Be one with rhythm of wind in tree,
One with rocking of ships at sea;
Hurry will vanish and cease to be
    In dreams, in sleep.

Wrapped in fringes of golden fleece
    Go to sleep
And softly step in the shoes of peace
    Toward sleep
And into that magical country where
Night has no chill, and day no glare,
Where youth has wisdom and age is fair,
    In dreams, in sleep.

The Bereaved

In the next room
in the low chair
in the soft dark,
are you there?

I do not ask it
when sun is laid
through the checkered window
in yellow plaid.

Then, love that is past
seems rich enough
and having had that
I can give you up.

But in deep dark . . .
In the low chair
in the next room,
are you there?

I want you there.

IV

HEREDITY

WHEN A SHIP
WITH SAILS
COMES SAILING,
I KNOW WHAT
GIANTS BRED
IT;
ITS KEEL WAVE-
CURVED LIKE
ITS FATHER,
OCEAN,
ITS SAILS,
CLOUD-WHITE
LIKE ITS MOTHER,
SKY

At Earth, With Wonder

He went through the dark door
almost all the way through,
far enough to see lilies rising out of ashes, and more
height and light than he had ever known;
and the trumpets blew
his name in welcome. But someone called
and he turned around
against his will—almost against his will—and held
from soaring into air and fair light, took a small step back to ground
familiar.
     Then more steps back. And now, spellbound,
he looks at earth as if at heaven, at men
as if at angels, drawn to them
but most to one who called him back again,
refusing to let him go who was almost gone.

The Winged Imagination

This is a strange night. Bright stars at the zenith
Tangled in angled webs of their own blue rays
Seem too far, too cold, for this bold bird to dream of.
But over the rest of the vast sky is warm rich haze . . .

Haze like the deep shade made by a tree in summer
With no points at joints of the leaves where light leaks in.
Gentlest floating of wing will bring the bird without tremor
To rest and to nest in that dark, nearby and easy to win.

The haze may hold great hidden stars. The bird unbidden
Sings, and soft air swings with echoings of the song;
Rhythmic the swing as ring of hoofs of a horse well-ridden.
Then echoes change to a strange half-silence that flutters long,

And after, to muted laughter it seems, and warmth enwrapping
All together. But never is needed flash or flush
Of light to mark the dark or to solve the hidden happy
Mystery of love, discovered in haze and hush.

Unconquered

Life hid in bubbled air seeping through the tissue
Of spongy lung into dark blood to make it bright
    again.
Life dodged through filaments of nerve. He would
    not issue
To be caught at a sore's crater where little deaths
    begin.

Life mixed with busy pusher-out of oval pearly
Horn at the fingertips. He swam with lymph, to flout
Discovery. In maze of blood, Life found retreat.
    The burly
Rib bones barred life in and the sly besiegers out.

Where was brewed body food in complex
    combination
Life found a laboratory, a secret place to lurk;
Life ate, was eaten in spirals of mutation
When bile and pancreas were at their chemic work.

Life stung the end parts of every sense. Caprices
Shook him. He melted into body heat. With pain
And ecstasy Life split himself into children-pieces.
Life focused all: himself, bright star of brain.

Death found him somewhere, though. Who was
    the suborner
No one knows. Perhaps Life grew tired of constant
    war
And showed himself weaponless at an undefended
    corner.
So Death won. But Life won, too: here are children,
    and the star.

Apathy

Alarm should shriek a hurricane and go
Ripping the roofs from our complacency
And unconcern at what may come to be.
This is a time when high strong winds should blow.
But there is scarcely breeze to fray a rose
In thoughts of men, and in the pleasant sky.
World-statesmen only flutter as they try
To fan mild warnings into minds that close.

Why does not Nature scream a warning, strike
The hearts of men grown lax, adrift along
A course between half-right and semi-wrong?
This is a foolish thought. No symbol like
A storm or calm means much. Men make their weather,
World-weather—who knows how or why?—together.

Triumph

Sleet pounds at sea and tundra.
A young bear trapped, alone,
Lies anguished, wounded.

In frenzy he bites at the fire
In his paw, gnaws through the bone.
The wind now colder and higher

Soon turns the severed furry
Lump in the trap to stone
And the icy flurry

Clots the torn leg till only
A trickle of blood flows to freeze.
Then the cub pushes up and gamely

Struggles to run. He prints threes
Awkwardly but he does run,
Does gain his den in the tundra,
Does cheat the sleet and the seas.

Stairs and Ladders

Stairways are solid, with steps and risers
Nailed together, set in a space
Predetermined, and leading only
From one to another certain place.

But ladders, cousins of stairs, are freer.
They lean against trees, barns, anywhere;
They are found at fires, in mines, on shipboard.
They are built in the first place, half out of air.

Snow Shovel and the Shoveler

Utilitarian flat broadbottom of metal
joined to a factory-rounded fragment of tree,
this shovel, is made up of two universal
mysteries.
Its parts are diverse though earth mothered
        them together,
inert iron and living upthrust oak.

The tool in motion links unlikenesses,
snow and arms of the man who powers the stroke.
In rhythm the three keep moving. Repetitious
the lift, the fall, the return, the circular swoop
of snow flowing out in a curve and one with beauty
of hands and the scoop.

Scalpel

To excise the ego's
disorderly tumescent growth,
a scalpel of grass, projection
of small and humble perfection,
is sharp enough.

Old Spring at Independence

No living man remembers when
This water was not cherished.
Perhaps Harahey scooped it up
In coppery palms, or his squaws dipped in
A thick clay pot or a mussel shell
Brought here from the river.
French fur-traders drank here too
When they parleyed with the Indians.
Rim of the spring was dust and mud
When the Santa Fe trail passed by it;
When cedar pails and dippers of gourd
And fine china cups from Boston
Took turns with canteens filled by troops
Who guarded the covered wagons.

The spring still wells up cold and clear
Today as it was in the old days.
We dip our picnic paper cups
And Time itself flows for us,
Time
     whole
         continuous
             in the flow of this living water.

Mississippi

This is a very tall river.
It goes waterfalling over

canyon-wide cliffs and sloping
rockslides, forever stooping.

At last in the tidelands with seven
broad deltas, its height comes out even

with its match in another dimension:
the breadth of gulf and the ocean.

Mind Goes

Mind cannot penetrate everywhere,
not to its own pit's deepest level,
nor to its neighbor's. But manywhere,
where-enough, mind can travel.

Their Shapes Are Like

Their shapes are like and that is all.

The leaf, its shadow on the wall,
and the skeleton leaf, raddled and warped
left over from last snowfall.

One leaf breathes for the living tree,
one is a nothing that seems to be.
The third was real but overspent.

Think of them all, make no lament.
They are as life, dream, death, the three.

Listener

Mary ran to meet the guest
Down the stone-flagged walk
But found him tired and slow to smile
Or talk
Till Martha served them still-warm milk
And crusty bread.
Then she began to cleanse the bowls
But heard what was said.

Did he mind her working? He glanced her way
Just once while he told
How the money-changers ran from him
Spilling their gold.

Mary (in robes that Martha had washed)
Starry-eyed,
The perfect listener, sat entranced
At the visitor's side
And hers was the praise when he came to the end
Of the stirring tale:
"Yours is the better part," he said,
Like any male.

Rise Like the Flood You Are

And there is Autumn in the wind, to lend
the attributes of water to it—eaves
drip water-falls of wind; among the leaves,
and in my soul, it mildews. I should mend
my warping roof and walls. I apprehend
my house may flood or fall when it receives
full force, the wind with Autumn in it, heaves
beneath that torrent rising without end.

Would it be madness for a man to think
that he could drown in wind with Autumn in it?
Or cowardice to say—Now wind, begin it?
It will be chill as from a glacier's brink.
I shall not struggle, nor my vow rescind.
Rise like the flood you are, submerge me, wind.

In The Dust Bowl

Reversal

Dust again. All our values are shaken
When earth and air reverse their functions, when earth
    flies upward and air presses downward, when earth
    is taken
And swirled in the sky, earth that should be massive
    and hard beneath our feet, and when air
Is a choke and a curse and a heaviness pushing despair
Under the sill and into the hard-pressed lung,
Air that is meant to be symbol of lightness and spirit,
    flung
Down in the dust.
We could not bear it except we must,
For all our values are shaken. What is earth? It there
    anything solid and sure? And what is air?
Is there sun anywhere?

In The Dust Bowl

We push through acres gone back to wire-grass bristle
To something faintly green a long way over.
Here some man dug a cellar by might of muscle,
Some woman planted a lilac, sole survivor
Slipped down in the pit. Who paid the heartbreak cost
Of living here, and the greater cost of leaving?
Even their path is lost.

After Drouth

The spring was no spring because the pall
Of dust was over all,
A winterish death to green of land
When the hand
Opened and gathered nothing.

After no harvest in fall after such a spring
If rain
Comes, however late, unfruitful,
Illogical hope for spring comes again.
The mind cannot cope
With the strangeness of this unwarranted swing
Upward. But even with hopeless hope
The heart can cope.
Itself is a strange thing.

Rain

We had known we should not really starve
Though the cows and the grass had died,
But we moved like sleepwalkers half alive;
Our hearts were dry inside . . .
Today when it rained we ran outdoors
And stood and cried.

Illusion of Fire

Wheelshadows from a neon sign
spin an illusion
of fire, where it is only lights that run
together, in cold fusion,
gaudy but thin lights, needing cat eyes
to use for reading.
They are symbols of how men now devise
flash for heat, and idolize
misleading.

How Guess?

I wish that I could understand
As well as my eyes can see
The blue miraculous bird which lands
On the green miraculous tree.

How do they guess, from nature's store,
To take what each needs, to be
Blue and winged and bird, the one—
The other green and tree?

Sleep Spell

Sway right, sway left,
  Trees, trees.
Blow through, slow through,
  Breeze, breeze.
Flow, tide . . . ebb, tide
  Go, come.
Beat-beat, beat-beat,
  Drum, drum.
Soar up, float down,
  Birds, birds,
Swing now, sing now,
  Words, words.
Widen, deepen,
  Stream, stream.
Hold me, fold me,
  Dream, dream.

The Seed

The seed whether knowable
As vegetable, as human, or unguessable
As pinpoint thought
Is hope.

So many plantings. So many sprouts.
All true to type without variation
Of consequence? Perhaps, but search:
Sometimes may be found
A sport, a strange wild
Longed-for
One-chance-in-a-thousand mutation
Into super-apple
Genius-child
Or before unheard-of word.

She Thought That She Saw Angels

She was half-asleep and she thought that she saw angels
Thronging low at horizon, crowding as if
They needed to elbow for room to come up over
The edge of the world with wings full of blessing for her.

They were not white angels, not ghostly, full of portent.
Some were butterfly-dappled, or pink as rosebuds.
Shiny as foil some of them were, and others
Had dusted starshine over their peacock feathers,
And all of them smiled.

Lovely, lovely, she breathed. Oh the changeful and lovely!
Rich and happy am I to be visited so
By angels smiling, floating with wings full of blessing.
Their smiles are light. Their wings are flashes of light!
And she came full awake, seeing the glory of sunrise.
And full aware, turned to the glory of love.